TERRA FIRMA

The National Poetry Series

The National Poetry Series was established in 1978 to publish five collections of poetry annually through five participating publishers – E. P. Dutton, Persea Books, Atlantic Monthly Press, Copper Canyon Press, and the University of Illinois Press. The manuscripts are selected by five poets of national reputation. Publication is funded by the Copernicus Society of America, James A. Michener, Edward J. Piszek, and The Lannan Foundation.

1990

TOM ANDREWS, *The Brother's Country*
  Selected by Charles Wright / Persea Books

THOMAS CENTOLELLA, *Terra Firma*
  Selected by Denise Levertov / Copper Canyon Press

DAVID CLEWELL, *Blessings in Disguise*
  Selected by Quincy Troupe / E.P. Dutton

ROLAND FLINT, *Stubborn*
  Selected by Dave Smith / University of Illinois Press

CAROL SNOW, *Artist and Model*
  Selected by Robert Hass / Atlantic Monthly Press

D1738457

The National Poetry Series
Selected by Denise Levertov

TERRA FIRMA

poems by

Thomas Centolella

Copper Canyon Press
Port Townsend

Acknowledgments: Many of these poems were first published, some of them in earlier versions, in the following magazines: *Ironwood, New England Review, Audit, Shenandoah, Blue Buildings, Five Fingers Review, Frank, The Practical Mystic,* and *The American Poetry Review.*

Copper Canyon Press is in residence with Centrum at Fort Worden State Park.

Book design by Tree Swenson.

The type is Aldus, with Meridien display.
Composition by The Typeworks, Vancouver, B.C.

COPPER CANYON PRESS
P.O. Box 271, Port Townsend, Washington 98368

CONTENTS

This book is for my family,
my teachers, and my friends—
many of whom have been
at one time or another
all of the above.

That year everything went transparent.
First the buildings. Their concrete and granite,
their monumental marble, all seemed like
cardboard facades one stiff wind would flatten.
Then faces. What they registered was never more fleeting,
and what astonishments lay hidden behind them –
space shuttle, sonata form, world series, mortal sin –
were, after all, only fabrications of flesh and blood:
perishable, pitiable, nothing more.
Worst of all was hope. Like wine
turned back to water, hope was weak
and easily seen through.

It was something of a miracle, then, that one day
when, dwarfed by the library's massive vault,
penned in by words intended for posterity,
I stared at the hand holding open my book
and saw it was only flesh and blood,
but perfect. The greenish veins, the knuckles
and grimy nails, the fine reddish blond hairs ablaze,
even the tiny white scar left by an army knife when I was seven –
my hand was nothing to be improved upon.

And I looked up from the book that had been failing miserably
to enlighten or uplift me, and among the dreary stacks
and institutional quiet, I was drawn
to human faces – each one holding the weight of a world
carefully chosen or acquired at random,
faces open to me now as any book –
and one by one, I began to read them.

HUMILITY

Humility is what they liked to teach you,
those peaches-and-cream-cheeked nuns,
but not by the golden rule. With a ruler
the sisters rapped your tender knuckles
in front of everyone, or bare ass in the cloakroom,
while the rest of the class, as guilty or not,
gloated in safety behind their desks.

In high school, the men known as brothers
forced you to stand on your own two feet
for half an hour, arms spread as in a crucifixion.
Your parents gave them the power to make you balance
on the back of one thin-wristed hand
the weight of the Old Testament. On the other,
History of Western Civilization.
Drop either one and a hammerlike fist would nail you.

But the old parish priest . . . Not sadistic. Sad.
His windblown hair aglow, he called it
his "disheveled halo." The advancing senility
your parents mentioned was not apparent to you.
At a parish breakfast once in wartime, lost
among the pillars of the community, he wandered
up to you and murmured, "If you ever
come across the word *Pyrrhic,* remember:
it means victory at a terrible cost."

And because you were greedy for perfection
every Saturday after lunch you'd eat humble pie
and go down to confession, and slip into your side

of the dark. You'd say, "Bless me, Father, for I have sinned,"
a Christian thrown daily to the Christians.
He knew you'd been mauled and believed in you,
raising his right hand to make the sign
that means *freedom from fear.* A little humility,
he'd say, can keep us healthy. "Pride goeth before a fall."

ZENO'S PROGRESS

It is always late at night and always the night in mist
when these paradoxes are felt the most.
How can the boy leave a life force behind
in that dream house of his, and make it back on his bike
along the winding brick side streets,
through alleys no wider than two shoulders,
if at any one point his Peugeot is not moving?

It must be agony, wanting as much as he does
to get away quickly as possible, and getting nowhere.
On our way home across the street
we study him as we would the still
from a movie at the neighborhood theater:
we know that inside, larger than life, he is moving

and move on ourselves. In a fog
that blurs even the streetlamps, the boy
is certainly not lit up. But the idea of being
someday beyond this impasse, of thriving
under a cupola that pinpoints Andromeda,
is a possibility seen in a natural light.

Though he doesn't seem to mind
his young life is caught in this freeze frame,
his hands and nose and feet are getting cold.
And with that reminder he's off again,
until the next light that will stop him and hold him,
he's down the road again, an arm's length from traffic,
hunched over the elegant bones of his bicycle,

his progress blind, surging, prehistoric.
While farther and farther behind him, two floors
above the street, a man gets up in the night
recalling how interminable those still points seemed
that got him here, and step by slow step
makes it to his desk to write all of this down.

THE ART OF CULTIVATION

1.

It's no secret what he's up to.
Bowing like an old Muslim in midday sweat,
crouched in overalls and orange tractor hat,
duckbill shading him from sunstroke,
he's up to his neck in the bushy green sprawl
of tomato, pruning what's gotten out of hand.

His young neighbor, a real looker,
sees what he's up to. She smiles weakly
and leaves him alone. Under his breath
he thanks her for that. He needs to keep his mind
on what he's doing. The pruning shears
are newly sharpened, can clip off a stalk
thick as a thumb.

Seven stalks sprung from a common root
climb for the light. Only one
will live to drink it in. Something grows
taut inside him, snaps
when six are cut for the compost heap.

But what's essential thrives in that one shoot
rising straight from the center
with original impulse. This
is what he must keep his mind on,
before it's too late. Off come
the dragging bottom leaves, off come
the lower forking stems, those suckers
that veer into space. Off with each little world
small as Mercury, red as Mars,
but too infested to cultivate.

12

2.

An afternoon in this steamy plot and it's hard to breathe.
The strong rays through the eucalyptus
are going horizontal. He calls it quits,
armpits reeking as of garlic, fingertips black
from pinching those damned leaf-hoppers.
He'll turn on the sprinkler, then go shower.
Let the garden laze in a steady heat,
simmer in watered dusk.

In a month, with a little luck and much élan,
he'll be baking eggplant in a thick red sauce.
The paper says not in thirty-three years
has hard labor yielded so little. Nevertheless,
he'll need some help to finish off the *parmigian*.
Maybe break out a new Chianti, invite his neighbor
who's too young to be a sulker and too pretty.
Stripped down to his birthday suit, he tells the mirror,
"If it's two, it's a party."

SANTA SABINA

He was tired. As on a long journey
you have only the desire to rest your head
on a companion's shoulder. Days went streaming by,
so much scenery in the window of a train.
At night the clock was a pulsing red,
like the warning signal of a flight
that must circle indefinitely
before it can land on level earth again.

He was tired as he never wanted to be.
Alone, immobile on a hard bench
facing a stone wall streaked with orange
where water had drained for two thousand years,
he couldn't say for certain how long it had been
since the others went on without him.
Wherever he struck out from there
he'd be a stranger asking directions.

The old men had to laugh.
They said he hadn't hit his prime
and already he'd got that look
of one who's left this life and won't be back.
And how could he blame them? What he took
for smiles at first, some provincial amusement,
was only time pulling their lips back
to where there is no laughter and no time.

He would get up soon. A few more minutes.
A few more days. Centuries.
Maybe go down to Santa Sabina,
take the road through eucalyptus
and yellow acacia, the convent women

bent over vine slips, tending the wine of life.
In their courtyard, an orange tree,
ivy on the arches, linnets in the ivy:

It might do some good to sit and watch
Mother Superior sweep the bricks.
To be present like another mute object
needing to be cleared of dust.
No more whining, no more excuses.
Just the firm steady stroke of a broom
and the bell, later on, for evensong.

NOCTURNE: NEW YEAR'S EVE

for Modestina Inglese
my Italian grandmother

Now I know why I felt so sad today.
Why this last day of the year I felt
like a woman on her last legs,
bending toward the ground, leaning toward her last appointment.
Now I know why the hours were a slow procession
leading to this mound of snow, and why as I went to rest here
I looked at the sky as if I'd never seen it before.

Lying here, I have no trouble
imagining the woman who's been everywhere
and says *Enough* in four languages:
English, Italian, Baby, and Silence.
Her body, always so prone to pain,
now feels celestial, feels like nothing
but what six or seven stars imply.
So peaceful to lie down and not be afraid
of all the degrees below zero.
So good to forget trudging through the blizzard
that erased everything once familiar to her.
Now that she's over the hill
she's becoming part of it.

Back in the house my thoughts empty out,
they drift from room to room.
From next door comes a fuzzy piano:
music to be ninety by, broken hip music,
music of the wispy hair, and a cloud
that inches from eye to eye. I love this
largo movement somebody's put on
an ancient phonograph. Even with the eyes closed
it doesn't sound like a dirge at all.

And instead of the woeful moon rising,
I see a good woman sneaking under a dirty apron
ice cream for her punished grandchildren.
She sports a puckered grin toothless as an infant's
that a prankster of a son is making fun of, but lovingly,
and the horned fist quick to curse him, but lovingly.
I can hear the cracked dinner bell of a voice
calling out for the last time, and the small bird
that survived a paralyzing storm
to roost in an old woman's throat, to nest
in her wordlessness through every kind of bad weather.

And now I hear that high-pitched hoot of hers
ringing in the new year. A laugh that always was
a slap in the face of gloom.

SITO

for Kazoun Acey
my Lebanese grandmother

That last visit, so much of you already had left your body.
Just enough of a voice stayed on
to say no to breakfast, no to dinner,
to ask me about my beard. (In Lebanon, the beards
belong to priests and other guardians of the faith.
In Lebanon, a woman in a white linen shift
is dreaming against a cedar, eyes open
as if in the postpartum daze of her ninth birth,
three dark holes across her chest.)

I said my beard was fine and complained you never taught me
how to make your *pita* bread. Too late now, Sito,
you whispered, calling me by the name I call you.
But I can still make the *leban* all summer:
yogurt flecked with mint leaves and the cool
slices of cucumber, green-rinded, like your eyes.

If we had lived in the old country, in another epoch,
when Lebanon was still Phoenicia, I might be giving you
something more practical to take to the grave:
an afghan for that chilly waiting room, a bowl
to mix your flour in, a candle to search the grottos
for grandpa. Still, the rose I place on your casket
will not fade. The priest said as much with his persevering
chant for the dead. I couldn't understand the Arabic
but I picked up on what he meant.

Sito, he seemed to be praising all of us, but especially
the ones who touch your brow with their lips,
your dead hands with their dying ones.
They stare into the coffin just long enough to see
your eyes moving rapidly behind their lids.
And your chest, how impossibly it rises with its deepest breath
as you enter an unfamiliar landscape, an irrevocable peace.

GIRL IN A PEASANT BLOUSE

1.

The first time I saw her was in a print by Matisse
in the high rent ghetto where students lived.
Summer night, and Lebanese hashish
was moving in a charmed circle.

Openness was everywhere. Windows, doors,
the way those in conversation touched.
Bodies had a life of their own. They'd float
or glide on the hardwood floors, they'd gravitate
to faces they took to be friendly.

I was there and not there: a ponderous weight
had sunk me in a corner, some numbing repetition.
It could have been the undeclared war
that threatened to last forever, or the red-haired woman
who had snarled in bed that I was killing her, killing her,
or the graveyard shift at the box and pallet factory,
buzz saws so ear-splitting I couldn't hear myself think . . .

And now I was sunk in an overstuffed chair,
one from another era,
its elegant embroidery worn away.

2.

Then out of the blue on the opposite wall
there is friendliness in a cotton blouse.
There are sprigs and leaves embroidered on the bodice,
windowpanes of dusk on billowy sleeves.
There are shoulders, broad yet delicate,
and breasts that would barely fill a hand.
There are hands that make in her lap a lock,

not of chastity but decorum. And a mouth
that intimates gladness. And eyes that flash
amusement. And behind the flesh
of her young face, a quiet resilience.

3.

This morning, on the advice of Marcus Aurelius,
against the disinclination to leave my bed
I told myself I would rise
for the sake of world order, for humankind.

4.

And spent the day suffering
the pretenses of the day, the required
performances, the practiced beliefs
we've all agreed are vital to our peace of mind.

Then home in time for the evening news.
A young woman being interviewed,
her story so extreme I think, This is just
more propaganda: two dead, nineteen wounded
among the scattered fruit of a marketplace,
and in retaliation she and her family
picked at random, dragged out of bed,
no leveling of charges, no interrogation,
taken to a deserted beach
where they tied up her husband, and seized
her month old infant.

They dropped the baby on a rock
and when the husband started forward
he was shot, point blank, and the woman
went all the way out of her mind:
her howl and her child's howl,
like nothing human.

So for the sake of world order,
for humankind, a rifle butt was raised
as if the infant's head were a trifle,
nothing more, say, than a spoiled cantaloupe.

    5.

I don't want to believe a word of this
but here is the commander who gave the orders.
It's curious: he has the same features
and same gentle demeanor
as the man who taught me humanities.

This commander was also reluctant to leave his bed.
Then the alarm went off in a clock
wired to explosives in a produce box.

He says, Everything that woman said is true.
And I will tell you why that child was killed:
it would only have grown up
with a gun in its hand or another bomb.
The many who would have suffered
have been spared.

And the child's mother?
Allowed to go, says the gentle commander.
So she wouldn't forget. So she and her kind
will never forget.

    6.

Back in bed with the *Meditations,*
I hear again my old teacher marvel
at how clear Marcus is in his resolve.
Here is a man, he says, in failing health,
campaigning against barbarians,
alone in his power at a bleak frontier,

who nevertheless triumphs:
if not over history, then over himself.

Sleep invades my body, it means to conquer me.
I underline what I can. Thanks
to my teacher: I don't forget.

7.

A different evening, a tiny kitchen,
I'm leaning on the countertop,
cool tiles the color of heaven.

In the building across the vacant lot
you can see dancers in exile, straining before a mirror.
On another floor, aging politicos, running laps
around the issues of the day. A few isolated rooms
give off the flickering cave-light of TV sets.
And on a lower level, a head is bent over headlines
like an apprentice over a workbench.

Later, after the last light's out, I think
of all those strangers joined in darkness,
I think of many bodies in a city morgue
or mausoleum. How close they are, and how ignorant.
What intimacy would exist between them
is just another dream the living entertain.

8.

Turning away and into myself,
I'm looking down into an ancient city.
There's the girl Matisse loved to paint.
She's older now. The days of striking poses
are over, and those godforsaken nights
tearing her hair on a bloodsoaked beach.
She's remarried, moved on, another name taken,
another beautiful child carried: her small part

22

in the war against despair. She's floating now
through Paris, among the same kind of trees
that lined her homeland's smoldering boulevards.
These trees around which the future
is always under construction, these good friends
that know from experience what she has withstood.
In this new life, no need to condone or condemn.
Past the Cathedral of Our Lady of Sorrows,
down the Street of Steaming Baths, and then
the Road of Straws where Dante quarreled in his student days.
She joins factory girls at market after work.
They're testing ripeness in their pale hands.
The late light on a crate of persimmons
is anything but *nature mort*.

     9.

She is the one for whom romantic love,
even as she embodies it, is not enough.
Because the world outside the lovers' world
tends to be diminished: the less than ideal life,
brutal, relentless, that means to prevail,
is dangerously lost in a background
of vanished detail and little perspective.
She has learned to care less
for the easy praise, the cheap guarantees
on which the weak depend, or the artful
gestures that would make her immortal.

Even so, she remains a figure of the festive.
She is the Highness who walks among her subjects
unrecognized in a peasant blouse. Sometimes
when I'm withdrawn, brooding over the latest threat
from invading forces, I get this look on my face
as if it's the end of the world,
and I'll look to her for confirmation.

Oh not yet, she'll say without a word.

PROLOGUE TO THE HAPPY POEM YOU ASKED FOR

I met a woman from Greece much older than you,
not so much in years, but something gone from her face,
a certain light, a certain music. Her lover
had left her. She's not the kind who can live
without love in the house. Sometimes,
I tried telling her, we have to do without.
Her face was white as a marble Aphrodite
whose ideal smile has been worn thin. She asked me
in her broken English if I was ascetic.

Sometimes I think like someone three times my age:
recall the foreign wars, the domestic rifts, insensate losses,
and still want to live a simple life rich in simple pleasures.
Remember the summer I talked to you long distance
not so far from the heart of the country?
I made bread for the first time that afternoon.
I can see the flour dust rising in the sunlit kitchen,
while up on the cupboard Vermeer's milkmaid goes on pouring
eternal milk in her own apricot brandy light.

This morning, a letter from the middle of nowhere.
"I wish to stop writing, for personal reasons . . . "
And my eggplant, my purple beauties, shocked by frost.
What I'm left with is wanting the best of everything
even as I let it go. To be as moved, and removed, as the time
I came upon a boy in the kind of red leather hat
I lost as a boy: ankle-deep in leaves, he was spinning
by himself a small merry-go-round, the rabble
of his playmates fading as they scuffled to dinner.

What I want is to know what matters, and not want it
too much: not only to crave little, but to lack little.
To keep intact, by grace or good luck, the importance of

24

equilibrium: the young museum guard's humorless "Don't touch"
followed by the radiant old guard, who worships the ruined
goddess of love, who shares your awe at the voluptuous lines
that remain, agreeing as the gallery goes black
that merely to look is never enough –
and reading your mind, discreetly turns his back.

EVIDENCE

Blizzard broke the city's back. A week
of no work and no play. Windows rattling,
wind chill factoring through the cracks,
visibility stuck at zero. For heat
I wore three turtlenecks, for sanity
scatted along with Monk and Bird. At night,
asleep, my daydreams took a turn for the weird:
from an eccentric uncle I inherit a huge sum
but never see a nickel. People want to know
am I wealthy or not, and I have to say yes
though lacking the hard evidence to make my case.
Next morning I thought of Raymond, one of my
young "disableds," all bones and bangs, I.Q.
that matched his feather weight. And unperturbed
that overcast Friday when the class psycho,
for no apparent reason, spit in his face.
Manic Floyd and I almost came to blows,
but equable Raymond – mucus dripping from chin
and nose, braces glinting like stars in an almost
beatific grin – Raymond said it's OK, crazy people
can't help themselves. When I asked him later about
his favorite things, and he said watching the Channel 7
weatherman, I had to wonder what crazy was,
worried he'd grow up to be one of those drifters
who checks pay phones for change, gibbering all the while
to himself. Floyd and Company were howling now,
kids on their way from broken home to Juvenile Hall
who'd spit all day on the claim the meek would inherit
their turf. I didn't know whether to laugh myself
or fear for Raymond's mild soul, his sad gift to be simple.
But when that poor kid said he was glad to hear
those highs were moving in to meet those lows,
light broke through the window right on cue,
conjured a gold coin from behind his ear.

UNIDENTIFIED FLYING OBJECT

for WC

1.

The elements, if not cruel, can seem inhospitable.
But the trail to the Grand Canyon proved
to be five kind miles of switchback:
just glimpses of vista, acclimating us
to the tremendous. At the North Rim
one-fortieth of that foreign space
was enough to overwhelm.
At least there were swallows, their aerial ballet,
one whizzing past us toward the canyon floor
faster than a hawk after a little snack.

We needed to return to a habitat
and Sedona obliged with its smaller scale:
Oak Creek Canyon, moss green pools,
minnows surrounding our waists
with the intense one-mindedness of a home tribe
circling the white intruders, but friendly this time.
A miniature waterfall chilled us awake
before we crawled, grinning like amphibians,
onto warm rocks. The dragonflies
would light on the back of a hand
just long enough for us to study them.

And one day, serendipity: a kind of trail guide
was provided us, a young woman named Lisa
who appeared in the woods like a doe –
eyes dark, limbs delicate, the center of stillness –
but unafraid. She told us of wild asparagus,
raspberries ripening, the blackberries rampant,
right there for the taking. She showed us

the tattoo near her left breast, a heart lifted up
by slender wings. The symbol, she said,
for lasting freedom. And later, bathing in the river,
"I feel so unnatural when I'm wearing clothes."

Desire stripped us of many pretensions
but we weren't wild enough to touch her.
She led us down to the apple orchard: Innocence,
I thought, leading us back to innocence
and not temptation. But we couldn't follow her
all the way in. We didn't have time,
that old complaint.

2.

Sundown on the interstate, we're creatures in transit,
alert, herding past the red of mesas, the blackish
green of chaparral. Not speaking unless in danger,
not stopping while the way ahead is clearly marked.
We just passed a ranch called *Back-O-Beyond*
and that's exactly where we are: long passed through
the looking-glass, far from our warped reflections.

And now that sudden sphere of light
too low on the horizon to be a star,
too large and bright for a planet – What the hell
is that? What should we call the widening beam
it emits earthward, and those swirling vapors
we've seen somewhere before? Like fumaroles
before the volcano blows, or the backlighted steam
of city sewers when passion is nowhere else in sight.

Is this what Lisa meant when she said,
"I swear there's real sanity in the open air"?

Now the tractor beam is swallowed up by its source
and the luminous mists follow, and it all recedes
into the depth of atmosphere . . . Much as we vanished
at the Canyon's North Rim, looking down
and down. And later dissolved in the desert's
middle distance, looking for that one site
where our spirits might lift again
and not feel so alien.

LINES OF FORCE

The pleasure of walking a long time on the mountain
without seeing a human being, much less speaking to one.

And the pleasure of speaking when one is suddenly there.
The upgrade from wary to tolerant to convivial,
so unlike two brisk bodies on a busy street
for whom a sudden magnetic attraction
is a mistake, awkwardness, something to be sorry for.

But to loiter, however briefly, in a clearing
where two paths intersect in the matrix of chance.
To stop here speaking the few words that come to mind.
A greeting. Some earnest talk of weather.
A little history of the day.

To stand there then and say nothing.
To slowly look around and past each other.
Notice the green tang pines exude in the heat
and the denser sweat of human effort.

To have nothing left to say
but not wanting just yet to move on.
The tension between you, a gossamer thread.
It trembles in the breeze, holding
the thin light it transmits.

To be held in that
line of force, however briefly,
as if it were all that mattered.

And then to move on.
With equal energy, with equal pleasure.

Big city, big party, and no one listening
to the woman overcome by bourbon
and beyond caring. The couple she's pointing out,
though not imbibers, seem further gone than she is.
Were they the planet's last survivors
there wouldn't be more passion in their kiss.
The lonely drinker leans on me and whispers,
"When two people fall in love
they go to the wilderness."

*   *   *

At the western gate of Glacier Park
the brochures gave it to us straight:
here, in this world, we were visitors
and were to act with propriety, as good guests should.
On Going-to-the-Sun Highway
we stopped now and then to honor our hosts
by paying attention. Elk. Water ouzel. Osprey.
A mountain goat, unearthly white, playing hide-
and-seek in our binoculars, foraging like a god
cloistered among the lifeless rocks
of the Great Divide.

*   *   *

The thought of grizzlies kept us close
and careful not to intrude on anyone's privacy.
We practiced the songs that would announce our presence.
At Clark's Summit, three hikers, arm in arm,
skipped past us singing "The Wizard of Oz."
Through Sacred Dancing Cascade a rainbow danced
and we each played at being the pot of gold at rainbow's end.
Then vegetation thinned. Air grew rare.

We felt rare, like the first of a species
or the last. In the middle of the trail,
a flat rock, reddish, shaped like a child's valentine,
and we sat down to catch our breath:
not for words or song; for breathing.
Later in the pickup we slowed again,
this time to pay homage to the Weeping Wall.
But its vale of tears was barely a trickle.

*   *   *

At night, we broke out beers, burned Douglas fir,
stoked the fires in the back of our minds.
Over our small talk the Big Dipper poured its spell.
Then it was old fear that spoke, our failures at love,
our wondering out loud if there was someone somewhere
we'd never run away from. Possibility flared
in the chilly dark, more a home fire than a shooting star.
I got lost in the wished-for richness
I saw rising in her face, half of it
golden again, retrieved, as from a cave-in.
She stared back. I wondered what she saw in me.

*   *   *

At sunrise, a gale tore at our orange tent,
almost blowing us away
in a flurry of cinders and orange-yellow leaves.
Seventy miles per hour of pure abandon
flushing her cheeks, her hair a blonde fire. And wild
strange sounds came flying downwind to us,
half human, half other,
but all of a piece: neighboring campers,
making light of the air's distress,
were mimicking the flight of two wild geese.
A mock cry at the apocalypse, or mocking laughter.
A rough song that would carry them
from this wilderness into the next one.

A thought has been rising and falling
in the grayness of the season,
like a freighter in heavy fog,
appearing and disappearing:
How is it we never tire of dreaming
we can be autonomous as the sea?
Or be among the swimmers
holding their own against the undertow?
And the body surfers encourage us,
the way they submit to the powerful flux
and are buoyant, transported
by what could just as easily destroy them.

I keep thinking of that woman in Godard's
Two Or Three Things I Know About Her.
Real love, she said, leaves us changed afterwards.
What happens after that, she didn't say.
I remember you were grateful, as so many are
given the chance to move on to something better.
Fog lifting, the tide comes voluptuous as a great love,
and tastes bitter, like what comes after.
Stunning turbulence. Like a brilliant smile
that keeps edging closer, and from which
I edge away.

ANTI-ELEGY

for TNH

There are those who will never return to us
as we knew them. Who if they return at all
visit our sleep, or daydreams, or turn up in the features
of total strangers. Or greet us face to face
in the middle of some rush hour street,
but from a great distance – and not in the full flush
of bodies that once wanted nothing more from us
than the laying of our hands upon them,
as a healer lays hands upon the afflicted.
There are those who by their absence are an affliction.

I imagine that sometimes in your dark bed
you still want to know why. Why the man
you were just coming to love, who liked you close
as he raced through the city at night, why
he had to swerve suddenly. Why he had to end up
on an operating table, dead. Why you of all people
had to live, to repeat this unanswerable question.

I could tell you about a woman good at ritual
who, hardly believing in herself, was good
at making vows the two of us could believe.
Then one day I had to drive her to an early flight.
The dawn was blinding. She was off to look for the soul
no one else could provide. But was this the way
to do it? She didn't know. She wanted me
to tell her. Tears down her face. And I kept driving.
I can look back and say: on that day, that's when I died.

Since then, you and I have had a hard time believing
anything could bring us back. And yet your brown body
breathes new life into a cotton print from the fifties,
and picks parsley from the garden for spaghetti carbonara,

34

and cues up Mozart's French horn solo, and fills up the kitchen
with the aroma of sourdough, and gets my body to anticipate
the taste of malt as the tops of American beer cans pop:
good rituals all, because they waited out our every loss, patient
with the slow coming back to our senses, undeterred by our neglect.
As if they knew all along how much we would need them.

THE CONSERVATORY

I can understand the tree surgeon hugging the tree.
He's a little cracked, for the usual reasons, I suppose,
not quite as repressed as the rest of us.
So the small life stunted beneath the bark
is his own. Physician that he is, he's healing
himself, any way he can. He knows this tree
has a root in an early grave. And believes it will mend.

And the teenaged lovers think they're all alone
eyeing the calla lilies and the magnolias,
then each other. The calla spadix reminds them
of a small boy's erection. The magnolia pod has dozens
of little labias. When it seems the world consists
of such comely forms in a world of their own,
I keep walking, and try not to envy these sensualists.

It's time to visit my witch tree again.
Leafless, gnarled, it's scary looking.
But deep into fall it seems intent
on being griefless: its November leaves
greener than ever, its bark said to provide
a remedy for bruises. Its eccentric plan: adhere
to a pattern of growth amid the usual losses.

Be favorable to bold beginnings, said Virgil.
Easier said than done. I'm still wary
from the last beginning. Nevertheless, I've begun
a vigil: wait for the ally who believes
endings make beginnings necessary,
and who's plenty bold. Enough not to worry
about how much to give, how much to withhold.

What you need more of in your life, I think,
are some elephants. I don't mean elephants
like the one I saw in Washington, summer of '74,
Watergate all the rage. That one was a killer storm,
a whirlwind describing a vicious circle
on the dirt floor of its pen. I'd never seen
under a roof anything as big as that
move as fast as that. Maybe it was the fury
of having been used to represent
a party with such duplicitous members.
But don't worry. For you
I'd wish a different kind of elephant.

I was thinking more of two elephants in an Indian miniature.
Their habitat is a room that takes its quiet from the lake nearby.
The artist, someone we'll never know but to whom
we should be thankful, has placed our friends
prominently in the foreground. The sky
is an idyllic baby blue. Though we are not babies anymore
it comforts us, this sky. Far
in the background, miniatures within a miniature, are
the gilt towers of commerce and religion and government.
And leading from city to elephants, a road
no longer than the lifeline in your left palm.
On it two figures of little consequence are out for a stroll.

Though their surroundings are lush and calm
they've been carrying on a debate for four hundred years,
a kind of love affair with duality.
The elephants are so amused they're not only smiling
but one has taken its trunk
and is feeling up its companion's derriere.
What powers of communication! A direct pipeline of accord

between the brain and the seat of wisdom!
There's a cheerfulness in the air: harness bells,
sensual laughter, the fondness that elicits
fondling, though they may be nothing
but overgrown infants, these elephants.
It may be too they know more than you think,
more than you will give them credit for.
They could be everything in your life that lumbers along
mindful, affectionate, easy going and assured,
if only you could remember who you are.

Under the iris of each eye she has that white space
that could signify murder one,
or sex, or ennui, and which the Japanese
take to mean constant sorrow. I never know
what she's going to say next. I'm not sure
she does either. Among the usual pleasantries
she says, "I always fall in love
with the wrong person. I just do."

At the best café in the city, an antidote
for unwise choices: coffee pitch black
as if brewed straight from soil, Florentine
cookies on a gold-rimmed plate.
And in the voice, a remarkable matter-of-
factness. "I just do, that's all."

On our way out, the proprietor and a cop
trading tips on the longshots, she lifts
two *ossi dei morti* from under their noses:
two sticks of candy, silver and jointed,
that a crone with a sweet tooth long ago christened
bones of the dead. "They taste better
when they're stolen." Her face lights up

but her eyes still look like my uncle's
in his final days. Someone usually so at ease
his life had seemed a kind of answer
to those who questioned life . . .
Then cancer of the bone marrow
and precious few choices left.
A self-made man, reduced to the point
of begging strangers for his death.

"Bite into it," she says, "hard,"
the hard candy in her mouth, her even teeth bared
like a skull mask on Mardi Gras
or Halloween. A macabre grin,
worn in celebration.

Some unknown factor elates us
in spite of ourselves. It's a given,
not a choice. It's dark and bittersweet,
this chocolate marrow, this brief time
people call a life. We bite into it
hard. We do this together.
A local cure for sorrow.

1.

A nobody in her own eyes, she would find streets
nobody would walk after a certain desolate hour,
and would fill them all night with her singing,
till she was empty by the time she got home,
having sung for no one, not even herself,
and wanting nothing better than to sleep.

Since she joined the holy order, though,
she sings for the love of God.
She's two people now, both of them full:
one is the servant of what she hears,
the other is the integrity of what comes
shimmering out of her mouth.

Now she paraphrases Thoreau to describe her life.
"Music is everywhere. Everything is always singing.
It's only listening that's intermittent."

2.

She was never a nobody, not in my eyes.
Her voice was untrained, but the sweet
high notes were rarely beyond her reach.
Her hands were strong and loved my back.
She sang while kneading out the knots
and my muscles would hum along.

And when she cried, from deep inside
the diaphragm, that too was a kind of singing.
Sometimes we sang duets, and afterwards
in her room: the smell of much needed rain.

And later when she left, a nobody in her own eyes,
and said, "I'm not coming back" –
wasn't that a song with a haunting refrain.

3.

I wrote her about the seals, how every year
they migrate to a sanctuary under the Antarctic.
They're singing down there and nobody knows why.
Scientists thought it might be sonar, a way
of detecting other life, a way of securing meals.

In fissures of ice they rigged lines of fish
and monitored sound waves for data.
They dreamed up names for the expected outbursts –
jackhammer, swiss yodel, evangelist – and waited months
for something new under the unsetting sun.

But each day and night brought more of the same.
Monitors blank. Seals quiet in their cathedral of ice.
And a host of minds that had missed their guess,
mirrored sunglasses giving back to the land
the glaring monotone of emptiness.

4.

It used to be, every Sunday meant going to church.
Now the only time I go is to practice my piano.
The director of activities, an old friend,
lets me use the Steinway in the sanctuary.

The stained glass windows are circular,
like the shape of God, no beginning,
no end. The pews empty, the altar bare,
my hands remember their child's game:

"Here's the church, and here's the steeple ... "
The fingers used to play the people.

They still do: in their repertoire
you can hear a congregation of prayers,

a collective variation on the theme of longing.
And now and then, a song approaching
a psalm, nothing but pure praise.
One night, working late, the Asian

janitor must have detected
a tone of desperation. I caught him
sweeping dirt that wasn't there
to give me extra time.

After the coda he waited a few measures,
then asked politely, "All done?"
I appreciated his good timing.
When I said good night I meant it.

Outside, it was April again and the air
was the warmth Vivaldi must have known
those long nights he wrote *La Primavera*.
Horse chestnut trees in bloom

and a huge bright face above them: round,
not like the face of God, but like
the custodian's face, humming back
to the dark planet a kind of lullaby,

a kind of answered prayer.

    5.

After the seals failed to bite, much less sing,
it was back to Stockton St., back to sing-song Cantonese
dipping through the air like a dragon-tail kite,
awnings cranked out over windows of fresh seafood
that would make any seal croon,
and boxes of finger-sized dried fish, metallic blue

like tin toys from the five-and-ten,
and melon crates, mangoes, a mountain slope of plums,
roast duck on a hook, steaming noodles and soups,
and X-rated fortune cookies, red blush
of rhubarb, green blush of cabbages,
and the herbalist jars of coiled snake and fetal deer,
and the suckling pig on a platter, carried above the crowd,
its maraschino cherry eyes like rubies for a royal party.

6.

Walking through the crowded market streets
where nobody knows my name or speaks my language
and it doesn't matter, where my eyes are not as almond-shaped
nor my skin as pale nor lips as full, and it doesn't matter,
I'm also two people now. One is taciturn
and goes tone deaf at the name of God.
The other is a jailbird: isolated deep in my thought
he knows the whole block I'm walking
is an undiminished bar of eighth notes
on the larger scale of the street. The whole city
is a divertimento, streets undulating back
to some overture of first creation I can't begin to imagine.

Isn't it a happy accident, then,
to learn that just around the corner
the World Theater is playing a movie
called *Anxious to Return,* a little corroboration
that our desire to be where we belong
survives our dislocations. And good fortune, too,
to have these market signs. It doesn't matter
what language they're painted in, they translate
to music for a thousand mouths: *Hing Lung, Wee Wah,*
Sun Sang in the narrow streets: bright red
keys to the city, passwords that help us enter
the province of the living once again.

44

AT THE DOLPHIN TANK

Here I am praying again.
I've come down from the dim blue-lighted roundabout
where creatures of the deep circle in moody tedium.
Give me these other blues, like an Aegean resort.
Let me be taken through this underwater window
and commune with the slow revolutions
the dolphin, though captive, seems to manage
with no effort at all. How is it able, merely
on a whim, to cavort with phenomenal speed
as if its weight (which can level a man)
were beside the point? Where does its tireless smile
originate, and in its languorous gliding by
where did it get that eye half-closed
as if on the edge of a human ecstasy? It's so
entrancing even the schoolkids have been reduced
to whispers. This is a far cry from the pout
of the sea bass, from the salmon ripped to shreds
by leopard sharks, this mellifluent torque
of the water god dancing. And each time it leaps, suddenly
out of its element, when it makes that dazzling
break into the empty world of the air,
something in the children leaps with it.
"Ohh!" they exclaim, "Ohh! ... Ohh! ... "
until even the dispirited in me, resistant as it is,
has to admit defeat, light-headed
in the dolphin's wake, the water
pale gold with bubbles rising,
like champagne.

MAGIC HOUR

1.

Years ago, house-sitting between jobs, between loves,
I was new to this neighborhood with the bad reputation.
I was baffled to begin with, frustrated, confused,
and then there were the Christmas lights at La Rondalla
all summer long, and sweets in a window that always said
"Closed." Giddy women talked a good game
far into the night. I walked home wary of shadows
coming up fast from behind. Dark mornings
I tried to look ahead. In the pennant race
the local team was a dark horse, coming on strong.
My sudden cheers boomed through the empty house.
After a day of hellish interviews, wondering what to do next,
I came back at that time between light and dark
photographers call *magic hour*. Two Hispanic girls
playing a board game on the stoop. Their heartbreaking beauty
more so because they didn't know. "We hope
you don't mind. We're playing *Clue*. It's a mystery game."

A mystery game.

2.

I lugged dirty laundry in a green duffel bag
left over from the days when the President would intone
"My fellow Americans, it's with a heavy heart ... "
The Bloods, in leather and sweats, holding up the prisonlike
walls of the projects. One asked me if I needed some "help,"
flashing a green bag of his own. A face that looked as if
he'd done some hard time, or never stopped.
Buddhists bought the brick warehouse across the street
and painted it red. The black spraypainted flourishes

of Latinos were back in a week. And gone in a week.
When our team got knocked out of contention
I hauled my clean laundry, my heavy heart,
nodded back to mechanics on their mirthless break.
The most we could do now was wait till next year.
I tensed up at the cold snap and when I heard
one brother snarl *nigger* at another, a dirty word
that had almost got me slapped when I was small.

I slept, when I slept, with a thin comforter over my head.

    3.

Every phone call was long distance, even the local ones.
I feared for the living things entrusted to my care —
coleus, goldfish, ficus — delicate clean lives
oblivious to bad connections, broken glass, the honorably discharged
in a brown bag stupor. Postcards from the tropics
came marked with sinuous lines, calm, like alpha waves.
Laid squarely on the street corner, a yellow-stained mattress
still in use. Making change, the Filipino laundry owner
mourned the murdered Aquino, but was thrilled to be in America.
The Hispanic sisters folded bedsheets still warm, stripped
to tank tops while quoting the Scriptures, no bras. Evelyn
and Lillian. Red lips, sultry glances, blue sparks from the prongs
of electric buses. A gust lifted my favorite shirt,
Evelyn gently retrieved it, but my lust kept billowing.
Magic hour escaped the lethal-looking alleyways
unhurt. I raised my eyes to the hills. Evening came clear.
Even-ing, said Lillian, in her soft Nicaraguan accent.

Years later, I live here.

MISTERIOSO

The more people I know and the more I know people
the more frightening they become. Everyone
has been damaged to near extinction. Everyone
has loved inordinately those they should not have loved
except in the most disembodied spirit of good will.
And everyone has been loved at some time or another
by the wrong people, or for the wrong reasons, or for reasons
that at the time seemed suspect, insubstantial.
And who hasn't been at the mercy of circumstance:
born under a bad sign, born with bad genes, or just born,
period. Timing is everything and some will never be
the right person in the right place at the right time,
no matter how hard or how long they try. Period.

When I carried these black winter thoughts from work
and got two blocks from home, I knew something
was wrong: a darkness literally fallen upon Mission Dolores,
streetlights out, traffic lights out, the corner stores and the bookstores,
the movie theater and the café, all closed up. It threw me
back into the old New Age notion that we create our own reality.
I quickly started thanking my lucky stars, as if their small light
would suffice, as if merely the idea would click on
at least one lightbulb again. Of course, it didn't happen.
Doing the dishes by candlelight in a cold house, the steam
warmed me by degrees and I recalled Katrina, my first California love,
telling me that when her ex-husband came over for dinner
he didn't mind at all doing the dishes, unlike me.
He was a conga player and the hot water kept his hands warm.
The other thing Katrina said that I'll never forget
is that she would love me for eternity, in whatever form.
It took less than a year for the veil to fall from that sweet illusion.
There was a man who readily agreed to be compensation
for all Katrina felt she lacked. He'd been after her since her married days,

she wanted desperately to be married again, I wasn't moving
fast enough, and that was the beginning of the end.
Five years since I've heard a word from her.
We are ghosts to each other now. Period.

Suddenly the power came on, the lights, the radio with Thelonious Monk
soloing on his "Misterioso," and I blew out the candle on the sink
though its radiance, pale yellow and flickering, had made the kitchen gloom
a cave of companionable meditation, like the grotto in St. John's
when I was too young to be disappointed by the mysteries
of the Church. The votive candles would cast deep shadows
in the Madonna's mantle, but she stood resolutely on top of the world,
the evil serpent crushed underfoot. One day after school, praying
for all the souls lost in limbo, I stared for hours
at her flawless face. Stared until convinced she smiled at me
for my devotion; I was young enough to believe she knew I cared.
I blew out the kitchen candle and Monk was playing all the wrong notes
beautifully, in that adroit, mischievous way that had made Katrina laugh
when she introduced me to his quirky syncopations, and saw
the bemusement they put on my face. Solo finished, Thelonious called out
for "Coltrane! Coltrane!" and his tenor sax took over, and it threw me
back to the bay window in our high bedroom, the international
orange of the Golden Gate Bridge in the far distance, and closer
the gold onion domes of the Russian Orthodox Church, made more golden
by the sun going down: a scene like a picture postcard of the absolute.

The last time a blackout hit, I was standing at the corner
of 24th and Castro, waiting for a bus with Rita and Theresa.
When the lights went out it was like one stage set being struck
to make room for another: Twin Peaks appeared as the silhouette
of a young woman's breasts against the more-visible-than-usual
constellations, and we walked to nearby Finnegan's, all dark wood
and candlelight, where Theresa introduced me to Jameson
shot by shot. I hardly knew Theresa but I liked her
because her hair was dark and silky and down to her hip,
and because in the power outage the city had been made less
a repository of systemized repression, and she was wondering aloud

why more people simply didn't recognize they were animals.
Life was a matter of basic drives – appetites – and simple pleasures
profoundly gratifying, but we'd wandered far afield
of the elemental delights. It looked as if the electric buses
would be down for some time, and fog was rolling in cold,
so we went for a hot soak at Elisa's little local spa,
and Noe Valley seemed more a village than a neighborhood
and this unexpected darkness our true element, familiar,
inviting, like the steaming wooden tub we sank into
without clothes or self-consciousness, and which Rita, sighing,
referred to as a welcome return to the womb.

I finished the dishes and St. Thelonious Monk rejoined St. John Coltrane
and I decided I could be thoroughly annihilated by all the pain
others had acquired before they met me and eventually
visited upon me, if I let them. And as I cleared the counter
I thought of Peggy-O, who relied on household chores to ground her –
Zen work, she called it – and Leslie, who when her heart was broken
did a lot of scrubbing around the house, snozzled on White Russians
and calling me at one in the morning "just to hear a human voice."
And I burrowed through the famous interminable strata
of papers on my desk, fancying myself an archeologist on a dig
in the quest for order and clarity, moving toward that fabled city
whose fragments once recovered and reassembled
would bear with startling relevance on the present moment.
And the thought of other allies came to me, like Kathy
who when love had brought me to a bad end, again,
insisted I go on looking, insisted I "go for the one with the legs
and the sense of humor," thus becoming my Guardian Angel of Leggy Wit,
and I thought of horny Alberto, my alter-ego, who once confessed
"A stiff cock has no conscience," and I thought how heedless
people seem to be of their power to affect other people,
almost as if they didn't trust the exalting, exultant
influence their attention is capable of inspiring
in the kinds of lives that are like one long blackout.
And when I managed to reach the final layer of debris on my desk
I found a quote from Rumi fresh as the day I taped it there.
"Why waste your time with those who don't know you?"

50

It was a question with the teeth of a guard dog,
with the vicious bite of truth. Knowing the truth
might set you free, but after that it's a daily fight
to stay that way. Next to Rumi's quote was a yellowing
piece of irony, an old flame's note that said
"You've entered places in me that have no exits."
I thought of the transmigration of souls – from one body
to another – and how far certain ones had crossed over
my border, as if seeking in me a permanent resting place.
Their reluctance to go further, to go deeper,
had been unfathomable at the time – and had banished them
to history, to the incorporeal, to the limbo of mere memory.
Once, they were so pitiably human I'd had the impulse
to protect them from every darkness, foreseeable or not,
including myself. But they were spectral figures now, hungry ghosts
tracking their dirt through the house, helping themselves
to my dinner table and easy chair, to my favorite side of the bed.
And somewhere far inside me, haunted as well as haunting, they still
nuzzled the household creatures that were stand-ins for themselves
or the children they yearned for. And still trembled at the despicable parents
who'd appear suddenly in my stern features. And after their bodies
had been profoundly touched – though they were far beyond my reach –
they still wept: in old pain, or ecstasy, or gratitude, or fear.

For a moment, I felt a surge again of something close
to compassion, an overload to blow the circuits of the ego.
I felt tempted to weep with them in a fit of reconciliation.
And more: I wanted again to rally their lost causes
in spite of what was lost between us, to front a new initiative,
to come out on the side of jazz and other joyful noises,
to endorse good Irish booze and animal pleasure, to revive
the hot whispers and holy cries turned cold as stone,
like names inscribed to mark a grave. I was annoyed
at having been annoyed earlier at the temporary loss
of power and light – it seemed unworthy of the faithless
I had wanted to save, including myself – and for a moment
I had to laugh: hadn't I died too along the way, vacated

whatever it is that makes life worth the trouble, abandoned
my body to its hapless agenda? I don't know how
we get taken out of ourselves, or how we get returned,
but I was back now. Back to being human, back to the old dream
of accepting the timely disclosures of love,
or what in my time has passed for love.
Even if the truth love brings can often be ruthless.

CHRISTMAS LETTER

The young black guys are hanging on the corner
in football jackets and Santa Claus hats,
while in the wash and dry the little black boys
are so father-hungry they come at me on their knees
like rock stars sliding across a stage, pleading
"Oh please please please, you've got what I want."
They finger my red plastic laundry basket, they snatch
my bottle of bleach, they giggle through these larcenous maneuvers
as if there is no one who won't succumb to charm.
And it's true I'm tempted to lay a quarter on each of them
but Grandma in the corner, big as a bear, growls them back into place.
They can rag white dudes like me all day long
but they know better than to fuck with Grandma.
Last load packed, I'm out the door, past Smitty's Transmission,
his small garage cluttered with the likes of gear shafts
and manifolds and countless oily intricacies
that, once displaced, now seem doomed to languish
where Smitty has scattered them willy-nilly
in his greasy blue jumpsuit, red watchman's cap and gray goatee.
Next door, in front of Gold Mountain Buddhist Monastery,
two young monks in gray robes and shaven heads
are conferring beside their brand-new Nissan 4WD,
which is white and squarish and looks as if
it could whisk you across the bleak surface of the moon –
from the Sea of Chaos, say, to the Sea of Tranquility.
The Monastery is also squarish, big and red, a kind of Christmas present
plopped into the threadbare lap of 15th Street. One night
I raved like a lunatic along one wall, while my friend –
judicious as they come – let me rave, let the dark
twister above my head spin in its funnel of anger
till the frenzy wore itself out. I don't remember why
but I was stalking the inarticulate at midnight right down the middle
of Albion Alley, "the busiest little street in the world,"
cars parked on either side of me and good friend in hot pursuit.

When I finally calmed down she told me how Buddha,
who was deathly afraid of snakes, wrapped a pit-viper
around his eyes, and kept it there till he learned
to see through the fear. On the way home I must have passed
three or four older men, each on separate stoops, passed out
or hunched over in their own versions of the Sea of Chaos.
I entered the long dark corridor leading to my place
and left the light off. Walked slowly, touching the wall
to feel my way like someone blind-drunk. I could make out
the dimmest radiance, the proverbial light at the end of etc.,
and I thought, "This is my life."

The winter rains have arrived with a vengeance,
the stoop dwellers have fled to the soup kitchens,
I've got enough cash in the bank to buy a few presents
and still meet January's rent on my two-room
den of iniquity. I should be happy. I think I am.
My new tack is to counter the difficult with a one-two punch
of right action and formidable restraint. Failing that,
I'll fall back on being a homebody. I still make a killer
lentil soup, and there's been some lovely company lately
to attest to that fact. If I have a complaint
it's the unnerving days when no one will meet
my open look – light years from your gorgeous town
where even strangers greet each other like old friends.
Bad temper, dark moods – what did you tell me once?
"It's all weather." Yes, and the affirming days return like sun:
chance encounters, long distance recapitulations,
pow-wows at midnight and into the wee hours, even a passing
smile in the street – these days of connection are the true currency
of our wealth. It might be all maya, as the Hindus say, all
illusion, but at the laundromat a teenager was wearing this button.
"Enjoy life," it said, "This is not a dress rehearsal."
She was fifteen, tops. Kids are that smart these days.
We all should be so young. Remember, not till we become as children
shall we enter the Kingdom of Heaven. All right, so I'll never
be mistaken for one of the Wise Men. Season's greetings anyway,
every season. Know that I love you. This is not a cliché.

The solar panels are up over the projects,
the edible dandelions sprouting yellow in the vacant lot,
clover coming up thick around a kitchen chair
where a two-storey house once stood.

It's early February but the Japanese next door
say it's the end of the year. Spring, they say, has come
to rid the soul of last year's demons.
There's no Arctic blast to argue the point.

In my courtyard I smell lilacs
where there are no lilacs.

*   *   *

My demon called last week.
Just wanted to chat.
On a rainy night in late January
even demons get the blues.

Topic of discussion? Oh, this and that.
Couple of tame jokes, the usual news.
If you'd been there to eavesdrop, no doubt
you would have been bored.

With my demon, what goes unspoken
is what provokes.

*   *   *

Some days are like this: you can't move.
Can't be moved. As if you've put down roots.
What growth there is, is imperceptible.
A slow efflorescence.

Then the camellia, out of season,
blooms for you. The cherry trees bloom
like something you've been meaning
to remember. And the Japanese fern

which all winter was thought to be dying
shoots up a new green stem that spirals toward the light.

*   *   *

And other days: the window light woke me early
but I didn't mind. From the courtyard
I heard a trilling, intricate as my favorite jazz,
and half-dreamt that bird to be

the return of John Coltrane. A sweet
modulation, loopy, lively, it followed me out
the door, down the street, and around the corner:
like my mongrel, Errant, who would chase me to work,

then wander off for days – they seemed
a lifetime – but would always come back.

*   *   *

The ingenious Japanese are making masks of terror
to mock the awful past, render it harmless.
I'll have to make do with my face
which is already a mask of intense equanimity.

Fumes of hot pitch in the air, and far off I can see
the construction cranes at Third and Mission.
They loom over the empty lot where Robért
lived rent-free for years, and well, in his condemned painter's loft.

You pulled a string in the mail slot; it connected
to a tin can at the top of the stairs: his doorbell.

*   *   *

Next door at the end of the year: the heads
of sardines, hung from holly branches.
And parched beans, flung inside the house
and outside the house. "In with fortune, out with demons!"

Instead of fish and beans, I use disappointments
torn from an envelope, read quickly, discarded quickly.
I say it out loud – "It's all clear" –
like the reassuring signal after an enemy attack.

"Clear." As when the trauma surgeon with his electric paddles
jolts the cardiac victim back to life.

EASTER

Every day is Easter, or ought to be. A triumphant rising
from sleep, from dreams in which you were dead to the world.
In which you were a melancholy ghost, haunting the city
as it used to be. A couple walking home at midnight,
languid, arms around each other's waist, heads bowed
as if in prayer, or defeat, as if they had come to know
they were not immortal after all. You shadowed them
like an anxious angel, like the purebred that followed them
everywhere, like the rapture itself that had brought them together
only to abandon them to their own devices. Two aimless people
with a knack for getting lost in each other, on course
for what seemed a party crowd, milling outside the great cathedral.
You wanted to give them something that would hearten them
whenever they turned to it, but the best you could do
was inhabit the old body they had always welcomed:
the Italian potter, still a shining example of his craft, a fusion
of the useful and the beautiful. The gleam in his eye a gift,
it excited them, made them curious. And you, pleased
to see them this way, said, "It's our Easter celebration,
the most wonderful of its kind in the world. You should go in."
In a thousand hands were lighted candles, in a thousand throats
the same hymn, and your charges rose on tiptoe to see
what force could gather this many and keep them together.
All they could make out were the backs of heads, the slow
apparitions that were tiny clouds of incense, and above it all
a huge aureole, an almost breathing diffusion of light
they knew wouldn't last the hour. Then they turned away,
too exhausted to be inspired. Didn't even bother to say goodbye.
Just turned to the willful days lying in wait for them
and the faithlessness few come back from wholly alive . . .

And you stirred in your bed sheet as in a shroud,
could feel the day raising you as if from the dead.

You were like the soul singer whose first thoughts each morning
are of juice and sex, the aging athlete who when he says
he's still hungry isn't talking about food. And suddenly
you understood: your world, though lost, was still there
to be redeemed. Bad dreams. Hard news. The cold fog you hoped
would burn off by twelve. And a ceramic mug from Umbria, shaped
and painted by hand: orange and yellow, bone white and blue,
its brilliant and uneven colors of breakfast
shades of the imperfect life so many still believe is good.

CREPUSCULE WITH KATHARINE

Six o'clock. She's closing the store
and I close my eyes. She's the manager here
and since I'm the close friend come to visit
it goes without saying I can steal her chair.
It's staying light later and she lets down the white
shades of rice paper against the dusk.
Against the hour of closing up
she lets down her hair. "I didn't sell one book today,
not a one." I don't have to listen for a kind of cheerfulness-
in-the-face-of-adversity. It's there. It helps
the long day settle its hours in me, like sediment
in a cabernet she'd go for in a minute,
like Monk's vintage hesitations on the radio
aging me deliciously. He's playing as if he's missed
his cue, forgotten what comes next, but it's all expert
anticipation. She walks over to the tuner, says
"Let me turn that up for you. For us." Yes, this
is how I'm tuned, by those who know what I want
almost before I do, who offer what I need
without my asking. The dusk deepens in me, opens my eyes,
and her eyes are the color of dusk, deepening,
as she phones her young son, her husband already home
from work. The way Monk's weaving up and down the keyboard
you'd swear he was drunk, or in love
or both. He pauses before each beat, he waits
as you would before the mouth you've never kissed,
the blessed heat of the body you're about to join
your body to. She says the jazz greats
"boil it all down to the basic beautiful."
We listen and don't mention the dutiful calling us
to our separate ways. Monk is playing
the warm dusk and everything within us
and beyond us
goes without saying.

GOOD MORNING, SURVIVORS

At 16th and Valencia there's the celebrated pit,
as deep as the building next to it is tall,
where fire expertly gutted the Gartland Apartments.
The street says it was arson for profit and on the adjacent wall
a friendly spirit has painted, "Good morning, survivors."
Addo says it sounds like what a d.j. would say
on some postnuclear graveyard shift, but it could hold just as well
for whoever wasn't incinerated in that other unforgiveable blaze.
The pit starts at street level and drops straight down
and we descend, me and Addo and dog Max, my guides at midnight,
half on a lark, half on a mission to defuse this morning's
and every morning's blues. Max's coyote blood keeps his shadow
ranging over the sandy, desertlike terrain
past mounds of neatly arrayed, curiously arrayed
garbage: running shoes, beverage cans, a car grill, scraps
of leisure wear and Cyclone fence – refuse collected
from disarray, as in a child's playroom.
Addo claims those tall stems with the goldish crowns are fennel.
Can I smell the hint of anise? It's a small wonder
I haven't lost the olfactory sense altogether
living in the city. Is this a rehearsal set for the future?
You go underground to smell the flowers and the flowers
are weeds? We drift past concrete pillars under the sidewalk
and suddenly we're standing in someone's bedroom:
two mattresses neatly made, a footlocker, a nightstand.
"Hi. Qué pasa?" It's a young visitor cross-legged
on one of the beds, just up from Ciudad de Mexico.
He's enjoying his new digs. I guess it beats to hell
huddling with five crazies over a subway grate.
He doesn't care our town's due for a big quake,
he's already lived through two. We ponder his good luck,
welcome him to all the creature comforts of Norteamerica
and wander on. I dub him Arriba. He's moved up in the world

as we've moved down. I have to admit, it's not so bad
in this huge cool open grave. It's spacious,
stars are more scintillant, a rusty service elevator
will whisk you back to the upper world, if only in your imagination.
And we've brought along protection: gray-haired Max
still flashing his fangs, his bite as sharp as his bark.
His ears prick up when an itinerant on the sidewalk
struts by with a toucan call to the world at large
and Addo responds in kind. In the future, if I have my way,
all greetings will be conveyed with lyrical spontaneity.
As if on cue, Arriba cranks up his boom box
even though we're saying good night. OK. In the future
many a goodbye will be expressed in dissonant chords
progressing toward resolution. The air waves will be charged
with cycles in which coming and going are reconciled.
Static will be quickly dismissed for clearer frequencies.
And kinships will appear on any corner, or under any.
They will serve as the best elevators we could hope for.

Whitman thought he could live with animals, they were
so placid and self-contained, not one of them dissatisfied.
I have lived with animals. They kept me up all night.
Not only tom cats on the prowl, and neurotic rats
behind my baseboards, scratching out a slim existence.
There were cattle next door in the butcher's pen,
great longhorns lowing in the dark. Their numbers had come up
and they knew it. I let their rough tongues lick my sorry palm.
Nothing else I could do for them, or they for me.

Walt can live with the animals. I'll take these vegetables on parade:
string-beans and cabbage heads and pea brains, who negotiate
a busy crosswalk and feel brilliant, the smallest act accomplished
no mean feat, each one guiding them to other small acts
that will add up, in time, to something like steady purpose.
They cling to this fate, clutch it along with their brownbag lunches:
none of us would choose it, but this is their portion, this moment,
then this one, then the next. Little as it is, pitiful as it seems,
this is what they were given, and they don't want to lose it.

The gawky and the slow, the motley and the misshapen . . .
What bliss to be walking in their midst as if I were one of them,
just ride this gentle wave of idiocy, forget those who profess
an interest in my welfare, look passing strangers in the eye
for something we might have in common, and be unconcerned if nothing's
          there.
And now we peek into a dark café, and now we mug at the waitress
whose feet are sore, whose smile makes up for the tacky carnations
and white uniform makes it easy to mistake her for a nurse,
even makes it necessary, given the state of the world.

And when the giant with three teeth harangues us to hurry up,
what comfort to know he's a friend, what pleasure to be agreeable,

small wonders of acquiescence, like obedient pets. Except animals
don't have our comic hope, witless as it is. They don't get
to wave madly at the waitress, as though conducting a symphony
of ecstatic expectations. If I turned and lived with animals
I'd only be a creature of habit, I'd go to where the food is
and the warmth. But I wouldn't get to say to my troubled friend,
"Your eyes are so beautiful. I could live in them."

Just me and the flies tonight. Saving the world
can wait till tomorrow. A garden salad's in order
and some chilled Chardonnay – as close as I'm going to get
to Paradise. When the smell of cilantro hits my brain
I'm a hungry fool on his way to happy.

If I lived in the actual town of Paradise
I'd be rocking on the front porch, beer in hand,
shooting the breeze. Ignorance would be bliss again,
if only for a night. A blissful ignorance
like that pale pleasure craft

at Baker Beach the other morning: so far away
it skimmed the horizon, but remained
tantalizingly in sight. A day when everything
seemed possible. Though nothing in particular,
no one thing to divert the attention, or detain it

from the pleasures at hand: the Pacific breakers
a translucent jade, and children assiduous in the crafting
of parapets on their castles. Sleeping beauties lay
with their backs to the sun. I had the urge to turn each of them
over, and see what intrigues might be dozing there.

Next day, sand was everywhere: in sheets, pants, my old blue
running shoes with a star on each ankle – loose grit
reminding me of my element. The closer to *terra firma* one is
the more *firma* one feels. After a long hike, I stink,
therefore I am. And not at all like an old bar

near West Portal called the Philosophers Club.
The motto there: "I drink, therefore I am."
I've heard that if you can't change the situation

try changing your attitude. Fair enough,
but I've never been one for chemical inducements:

the inducements, God knows, are everywhere.
Not a year goes by that I fail to be chagrined
by how much I thought I knew the year before.
It yields that uneasy feeling again
of having little solid ground to stand on –

no metaphor here in earthquake country
and no joke: in a climate this temperate
a calmness inheres, lovers strolling the Golden Gate,
sunbathers in December, a willful ignorance
to get through the day – but it all disappears

when your building goes into convulsions like somebody possessed.
Late-night aftershocks will shake you awake
and leave you shaken. And leave you awake:
you don't soon forget how easy it would be
to enter the tribes of the dispossessed, a nomad suddenly

adrift in the dark city, blocks without water or heat,
no one with any power, except what can be summoned
from within. What doesn't kill me makes me stronger?
What kind of life would it be without those
we've spent a lifetime learning to be part of?

And another shock after the last big temblor:
bad as it was, it wasn't The Big One.
We were being given, again, our most difficult lesson
as though we'd only learned it by rote: nothing's forever.
All the more reason, some would say, to go back to sleep,

go back to work. And let the games begin again:
we need our play, the felicities of let's pretend,
the pleasure-flow between flesh and spirit

that leads us, on our best days, to our reason for being:
to become residents of the state of grace, legendary

principality, where time is not of the essence,
home is wherever we happen to be, and the day to day
life becomes us, like a beautiful coat we love
to death. When the saint advises, "Live in the world
but don't be of it," it makes me wonder: What happens

to the world? Does it suffer from our detachment?
Do we? Does life become an interval of bliss
between birth and death – or merely, as Cioran says,
"a ghostly parade of sensations"?
I used to think ignorance would be bliss

if total: if we were ignorant even of our ignorance,
as animals are said to be. Or had the knack
of ignoring it, as if it were true after all
that what we don't know, or don't care to know,
won't hurt us – at millennium's end,

a dubious line of reasoning, and dangerous
because obsolete. Even our paragon of genius,
Professor Einstein, suffered from ignorance.
The word *science* derives from the Latin
for *knowledge*, but as *E* became equal

to *mc²*, it's likely the great scientist
had no inkling of the fall-out to come,
no prescience. Not till many years later,
after Hiroshima and Nagasaki, did Einstein admit
to his "one great mistake." Our sad-eyed advocate of order,

didn't he suspect the chain reaction that split the atom
began in the Garden? Began with the first scientists, doomed
not by the craving for knowledge, or progress,

but power – and everyone after, forced into the breach
between self-preservation and the love of peace.

What if Nature had put me instead of Einstein
on the verge of relativity, knowing what I know now?
I'm the one assessing the calculations, tinkering with time,
the elements of the formula coalescing like a charm,
as if by some supernatural directive . . .

And I put down the pencil or piece of chalk
and slip on a baggy sweater, and take a little walk through
the vegetable garden. I chew on a mint leaf or two,
check up on the scallions and basil, the shock
of rocket lettuce, the not-yet-flowering zucchini.

I run my eye over this green schema
of the future, and think of the sympathetic magic
my mother might work with olive oil
and a little garlic. Then I foresee a blazing
Sunday afternoon, the scream of naked children on a dead run

through the backyard sprinkler. Older girls
in the pool fill out their new suits nicely,
and the boys are coaxing the men to play whiffle ball,
eager to show their elders what they can do:
smack the long ball, throw the wicked curve

my brain will register as a flow chart
of the finite, an arc breaking sharply from youth
to death. Women deliver dish after dish
to the picnic tables, a procession that seems timeless
and thus reassuring, even if I do know better.

For twenty minutes or so, all the griefs of relatives
are banished from the table, and I'm content over dessert
to forget I ever heard the word *nuclear*

in a context other than family. I'm content
to watch my young cousins slink away for the woods,

each secretly titillated by the other's new dimensions,
and smoothly shifting modes, I think: Gravity cannot be held responsible
for people falling in love. Or falling from grace . . .
As they head for their private Eden, I watch their long-limbed
backlighted bodies cut through my garden,

and I let them.

THE PRESENT CONTINUOUS

> Never forget you are a son of the King.
> —MARTIN BUBER

Dear Brother, I'm lying in the present moment
as in the bed I've made for myself
and here is the dream I'm trying to keep
from evaporating: it's second grade again.
The powers that be have made me small for my age
but I don't need to prove nothin' to nobody.
The bullies keep coming anyway, and I meet them
head-on. My wit is switchblade quick, my right hook
wicked. A few tough fights and I've made my name.
The nuns are bullies too—for them the world is like
the clothes they wear, everything is black and white—
but maybe they're only victims of the kind of bad choice
I'm determined to avoid. There is a young priest
who's Marcello Mastroianni in a collar and cassock.
All the girls hop to him like squirrels to Saint Francis.
He teases me about the rakish lock over my forehead—
it's 1959 and Elvis reigns supreme—and the girls turn
their seraphic faces toward mine, and it's as if glory
has been conferred upon me, as if suddenly
I've been declared a son of the King.

When your turn came you had everything to prove
and nothing to gain. A wicked right hand, a wicked mouth—
not enough. Enter tailored suits and a second-hand Cadillac—
still not enough. Enter bad choices abounding
in the guise of good ones, and both Father Marcello
and Saint Francis dead, gone to a heaven of storybook crap.
If you believed anything it was that you were not a son
of the wise and the powerful, but of the naive.
They lived in a dead end town, and if you took deadly risks daily

to escape, to enter the good life that always glittered
somewhere down the road, they didn't know about it,
or didn't want to know . . . Now you're languishing in the present moment
as in the bed you've made for yourself: a hard and narrow thing
riveted in place by laws you dismissed with an arrogant laugh
as if you were king. Now you liken yourself to a secret agent:
the state has given you a number and taken away your name.
The name you would have made for yourself,
the dream we all need to carry us from one day
to the next. From your penitentiary cell you write
that being conscious is such a deadening routine
your only moments of true life come in sleep or fantasy.
Now that you have awakened from the nightmare
of history, you lack a new dream to take its place.

What can I tell you that I haven't already?
In other dreams I'm my present age
but you're still a kid digging in at the plate,
the game on the line, those who love you
rooting themselves hoarse. I'm exhorting you
not to get ahead of yourself, not to go reaching
when you should stay back and wait. I know it's tough.
I know you're someone eager to make contact,
who lives for this chance in the green and gold moment
of a summer evening, your mind fixed on a dream
of a fastball, the sweet majestic crack of the bat
that lifts the world to its feet, that has everyone
holding their breath – and all your power, everything
you would be, driven deep, curving toward the pole
that divides fair from foul.

FOG LIGHT

for PYJ

1.

After her young boy toppled the boiling kettle,
after she cradled him en route to the emergency room
with his two year old flesh sliding under her hands,
after the doctor wrapped his arm to look like a mummy's limb
in the first stages of preparation for the afterlife, and even
morphine was cold comfort for the fire he begged her to extinguish,
she left husband and daughter at home, and ran out
to her mountain: ran the winding access road, the shifting grades,
the unpaved stony surface that will turn blisters into callouses,
ran till her lungs felt a fire of their own
and she fell, hard, like someone love has overwhelmed
and drained of resistance. And she lay there as if in bed,
the pebbles under her cheek cool as linen, a sleepy murmur
in the larches overhead, but where she broke the fall
her palms burning, and for a long time the waves
would not stop breaking through the length of her:
as if, like a lover, grief had come to know her body that well.

2.

Now fog has socked us in on her favorite trail, mother, son and me.
The larches are vying with the tamaracks for our attention,
a toss-up between fireball orange and saffron yellow.
If the leaves of Oregon grape, tiny and dark red, resemble
drops of bird blood splattered at our feet, she is careful not to say so.
At the edge of her neighbor's sixty acres, the gray air
glows coolly – the afterlife as dreamed by an ancient Egyptian.
Fog light, she calls it. It's like being inside a pearl.
When we spot the once innocent, now infamous
soup kettle, nestled in the undergrowth, it glows too
though it's badly dented, as if fallen from a severe height,

like space junk homesick for wheat grass. The path
is so wild in places her child has to ask,
Are we still on the path? Yes, honey, she says.
Where is it? he asks, and she answers like the patron saint
of patience she sometimes is, this woman who made me promise
I would never pity her. Where is the path?
You're right on it, she says. In the fog light
her boy laughs, scarred, beautiful, and reassured,
and laughing with him we turn home
as the rough path we love makes us turn.

PLUMOSA

It's tempting to chalk up the last seven years
to bad luck. From atop the refrigerator, the goddess of mercy
doesn't agree. She doesn't disagree, either. Who cares
if her left hand was lost in the last house move –
she presides over the household, cool as freon,
right hand open like a lotus blossom. And Tomu,
the Japanese fern that bears my nickname, Tomu
is still going strong, green polymorph changing form
as I've been changed. For a while two of its central stems
were bowed toward each other, a heart-shape
like a woman's beautiful bottom turned upside down.
But I haven't seen those ripe curves in months.
Ever since the stems went their separate ways
I've been daring myself not to make too much of it.
It's about time I employed my will
as a surgical instrument, excising with calm precision
the letdowns from various other changes of heart.
Is there anything alive that can be trusted
not to disappoint? Even the fern, whose wild aspect
delights, has nearly hidden thorns that can cut
surprisingly deep. I have you to thank for teaching me
its true name: *Plumosa*, which sounds like "plume"
but looks like "plum," a word that leads me out my livingroom,
across the bay, and down a street in North Berkeley.
Warm morning, no traffic, a neighborhood nicknamed
the Gourmet Ghetto. A man in a raincoat that has seen better days
is walking as if through water, wading through the murk,
the shallows of middle age. Plum trees line the block,
the plums blood-red, plump, succulent flesh.
He's muttering lines from the Good Book,
both volumes, the Old and the New. "I need to be given

a mouth and wisdom." A pause and then,
"By your endurance you will gain your lives."
He stops under a low branch of plums: ripe curves
primed for the teeth, the lips, the tongue.
He reaches up. Sometimes it's this simple.
"Sustenance," he says. "Sustenance."

TASK

He stands in the shower, a serious angel.
Finger and thumb at the bridge of his nose,
water steaming down the beautiful back
no one but God loves day in and day out.
He thinks: Something is missing, something that,
if it were present, would render my presence
unnecessary. The soap smells of cassis and he glides it
over the sore points on his trapezius
where powerful wings were pinioned once.
Life now is a more commonplace fall from grace:
eat food but don't taste it; play music
but don't hear it; indulge the self-centered
and call it commerce . . . It's not a savior the world needs
but a savoring spirit, a way to relish what's already
begun to vanish. The shower is warm and moist
and he just wants to stay put for a small eternity,
let someone else wrestle with the evanescent.
But he has his orders, which, once issued, can't be revoked:
Recover the taken-for-granted. That's why he hovers
above a child's gouache, a summer dress, the grass-fragrant
symmetry of playing fields. Why he's drawn to running water,
a birthday wish, the crackled glaze of celadon.
Why he exults in the power a silent moment wields,
and the number two, and the sweet word *yes.*
Open his notebook and you'll find disconsolate souls
who shuffle through the maze of their second childhood
whispering his name. You'll find pennies on the sidewalk
even the poor ignore. Skylights are there and scaffolds,
and desires in the dead of night concealed from the day,
and the ebb and flow that only happens
after certain secrets have been revealed . . . It's his mission
to protect all this from the tyranny of indifference.
When he wipes steam from the mirror, a face appears

and his task continues. Pierced ear, cheekbone,
a line near the mouth when he smiles
some take for adorable, some for diabolical –
a thoroughly human face he accepts as his own,
that he carries through the streets like a photograph,
wanting to say to whoever will listen: Have you seen
this missing person? Do you recognize this individual?
Take your time, look closely – and I can go home.